This
Bridal Shower Guest Book
Belongs To:

_____

_____

_____

Name & Relationship

_____
_____
_____

Wishes

_____
_____
_____
_____

Thoughts

_____
_____
_____
_____

Name & Relationship

_____

_____

_____

Wishes

_____

_____

_____

Thoughts

_____

_____

_____

Guest

Name & Relationship

_____
_____
_____

Wishes

_____
_____
_____
_____

Thoughts

_____
_____
_____
_____

Name & Relationship

_____

_____

_____

Wishes

_____

_____

_____

_____

Thoughts

_____

_____

_____

_____

Guest

Name & Relationship

_____

_____

_____

Wishes

_____

_____

_____

Thoughts

_____

_____

_____

_____

Guest

Name & Relationship

_____
_____
_____

Wishes

_____
_____
_____
_____

Thoughts

_____
_____
_____
_____

Name & Relationship

_____

_____

_____

Wishes

_____

_____

_____

Thoughts

_____

_____

_____

_____

Guest

Name & Relationship

_____
_____
_____

Wishes

_____
_____
_____

Thoughts

_____
_____
_____
_____

Guest

Name & Relationship

_____

_____

_____

Wishes

_____

_____

_____

Thoughts

_____

_____

_____

_____

Name & Relationship

_____

_____

_____

Wishes

_____

_____

_____

_____

Thoughts

_____

_____

_____

_____

Name & Relationship

_____

_____

_____

Wishes

_____

_____

_____

Thoughts

_____

_____

_____

_____

Guest

Name & Relationship

_____
_____
_____

Wishes

_____
_____
_____
_____

Thoughts

_____
_____
_____
_____

Guest

Name & Relationship

_____

_____

_____

Wishes

_____

_____

_____

_____

Thoughts

_____

_____

_____

_____

Name & Relationship

_____

_____

_____

Wishes

_____

_____

_____

Thoughts

_____

_____

_____

_____

Guest

Name & Relationship

_____
_____
_____

Wishes

_____
_____
_____
_____

Thoughts

_____
_____
_____
_____

Guest

Name & Relationship

_____
_____
_____

Wishes

_____
_____
_____
_____

Thoughts

_____
_____
_____
_____

Guest

Name & Relationship

_____
_____
_____

Wishes

_____
_____
_____

Thoughts

_____
_____
_____
_____

Name & Relationship

_____

_____

_____

Wishes

_____

_____

_____

Thoughts

_____

_____

_____

_____

Name & Relationship

_____

_____

_____

Wishes

_____

_____

_____

Thoughts

_____

_____

_____

_____

Name & Relationship

_____

_____

_____

Wishes

_____

_____

_____

_____

Thoughts

_____

_____

_____

_____

Guest

Name & Relationship

_____
_____
_____

Wishes

_____
_____
_____
_____

Thoughts

_____
_____
_____
_____

Name & Relationship

_____

_____

_____

Wishes

_____

_____

_____

_____

Thoughts

_____

_____

_____

_____

Guest

Name & Relationship

_____

_____

_____

Wishes

_____

_____

_____

_____

Thoughts

_____

_____

_____

_____

Name & Relationship

_____
_____
_____

Wishes

_____
_____
_____
_____

Thoughts

_____
_____
_____
_____

Guest

Name & Relationship

_____

_____

_____

Wishes

_____

_____

_____

Thoughts

_____

_____

_____

Guest

Name & Relationship

_____

_____

_____

Wishes

_____

_____

_____

_____

Thoughts

_____

_____

_____

_____

Guest

Name & Relationship

_____
_____
_____

Wishes

_____
_____
_____
_____

Thoughts

_____
_____
_____
_____

Guest

Name & Relationship

_____
_____
_____

Wishes

_____
_____
_____
_____

Thoughts

_____
_____
_____
_____

Guest

Name & Relationship

_____
_____
_____

Wishes

_____
_____
_____

Thoughts

_____
_____
_____

Name & Relationship

_____

_____

_____

Wishes

_____

_____

_____

_____

Thoughts

_____

_____

_____

_____

Guest

Name & Relationship

_____

_____

_____

Wishes

_____

_____

_____

Thoughts

_____

_____

_____

Guest

Name & Relationship

_____

_____

_____

Wishes

_____

_____

_____

_____

Thoughts

_____

_____

_____

_____

Guest

Name & Relationship

_____

_____

_____

Wishes

_____

_____

_____

_____

Thoughts

_____

_____

_____

_____

Name & Relationship

_____
_____
_____

Wishes

_____
_____
_____
_____

Thoughts

_____
_____
_____
_____

Guest

Name & Relationship

_____
_____
_____

Wishes

_____
_____
_____
_____

Thoughts

_____
_____
_____
_____

Name & Relationship

_____

_____

_____

Wishes

_____

_____

_____

_____

Thoughts

_____

_____

_____

_____

Name & Relationship

_____

_____

_____

Wishes

_____

_____

_____

_____

Thoughts

_____

_____

_____

_____

Name & Relationship

_____
_____
_____

Wishes

_____
_____
_____
_____

Thoughts

_____
_____
_____
_____

Name & Relationship

_____
_____
_____

Wishes

_____
_____
_____
_____

Thoughts

_____
_____
_____
_____

Name & Relationship

_____
_____
_____

Wishes

_____
_____
_____
_____

Thoughts

_____
_____
_____
_____

Guest

Name & Relationship

_____

_____

_____

Wishes

_____

_____

_____

Thoughts

_____

_____

_____

_____

Name & Relationship

_____

_____

_____

Wishes

_____

_____

_____

_____

Thoughts

_____

_____

_____

_____

Name & Relationship

_____

_____

_____

Wishes

_____

_____

_____

Thoughts

_____

_____

_____

_____

Name & Relationship

_____
_____
_____

Wishes

_____
_____
_____
_____

Thoughts

_____
_____
_____
_____

Guest

Name & Relationship

_____
_____
_____

Wishes

_____
_____
_____
_____

Thoughts

_____
_____
_____
_____

Name & Relationship

_____

_____

_____

Wishes

_____

_____

_____

_____

Thoughts

_____

_____

_____

_____

Name & Relationship

_____

_____

_____

Wishes

_____

_____

_____

_____

Thoughts

_____

_____

_____

_____

Name & Relationship

_____
_____
_____

Wishes

_____
_____
_____
_____

Thoughts

_____
_____
_____
_____

Name & Relationship

_____

_____

_____

Wishes

_____

_____

_____

Thoughts

_____

_____

_____

Guest

Name & Relationship

_____
_____
_____

Wishes

_____
_____
_____
_____

Thoughts

_____
_____
_____
_____

Name & Relationship

_____
_____
_____

Wishes

_____
_____
_____
_____

Thoughts

_____
_____
_____
_____

Name & Relationship

_____
_____
_____

Wishes

_____
_____
_____
_____

Thoughts

_____
_____
_____
_____

Name & Relationship

_____

_____

_____

Wishes

_____

_____

_____

_____

Thoughts

_____

_____

_____

_____

Name & Relationship

_____
_____
_____

Wishes

_____
_____
_____

Thoughts

_____
_____
_____

Name & Relationship

_____
_____
_____

Wishes

_____
_____
_____
_____

Thoughts

_____
_____
_____
_____

Name & Relationship

_____

_____

_____

Wishes

_____

_____

_____

_____

Thoughts

_____

_____

_____

_____

Guest

Name & Relationship

_____
_____
_____

Wishes

_____
_____
_____

Thoughts

_____
_____
_____
_____

Name & Relationship

_____
_____
_____

Wishes

_____
_____
_____
_____

Thoughts

_____
_____
_____
_____

Name & Relationship

_____
_____
_____

Wishes

_____
_____
_____
_____

Thoughts

_____
_____
_____
_____

Guest

Name & Relationship

_____

_____

_____

Wishes

_____

_____

_____

_____

Thoughts

_____

_____

_____

_____

Guest

Name & Relationship

_____

_____

_____

Wishes

_____

_____

_____

Thoughts

_____

_____

_____

_____

Guest

Name & Relationship

_____

_____

_____

Wishes

_____

_____

_____

_____

Thoughts

_____

_____

_____

_____

Name & Relationship

_____

_____

_____

Wishes

_____

_____

_____

Thoughts

_____

_____

_____

Guest

Name & Relationship

_____

_____

_____

Wishes

_____

_____

_____

_____

Thoughts

_____

_____

_____

Name & Relationship

_____
_____
_____

Wishes

_____
_____
_____
_____

Thoughts

_____
_____
_____
_____

Guest

Name & Relationship

_____

_____

_____

Wishes

_____

_____

_____

_____

Thoughts

_____

_____

_____

_____

Guest

Name & Relationship

_____

_____

_____

Wishes

_____

_____

_____

_____

Thoughts

_____

_____

_____

_____

Guest

Name & Relationship

_____

_____

_____

Wishes

_____

_____

_____

Thoughts

_____

_____

_____

Guest

Name & Relationship

_____
_____
_____

Wishes

_____
_____
_____

Thoughts

_____
_____
_____
_____

Name & Relationship

_____

_____

_____

Wishes

_____

_____

_____

_____

Thoughts

_____

_____

_____

_____

Guest

Name & Relationship

_____

_____

_____

Wishes

_____

_____

_____

_____

Thoughts

_____

_____

_____

_____

Guest

Name & Relationship

_____

_____

_____

Wishes

_____

_____

_____

_____

Thoughts

_____

_____

_____

_____

Guest

Name & Relationship

_____
_____
_____

Wishes

_____
_____
_____

Thoughts

_____
_____
_____

Guest

Name & Relationship

_____
_____
_____

Wishes

_____
_____
_____
_____

Thoughts

_____
_____
_____
_____
_____

Name & Relationship

_____
_____
_____

Wishes

_____
_____
_____

Thoughts

_____
_____
_____

Guest

Name & Relationship

_____

_____

_____

Wishes

_____

_____

_____

Thoughts

_____

_____

_____

Guest

Name & Relationship

_____
_____
_____

Wishes

_____
_____
_____

Thoughts

_____
_____
_____

Name & Relationship

_____

_____

_____

Wishes

_____

_____

_____

_____

Thoughts

_____

_____

_____

_____

Guest

Name & Relationship

_____
_____
_____

Wishes

_____
_____
_____
_____

Thoughts

_____
_____
_____
_____

Guest

Name & Relationship

_____

_____

_____

Wishes

_____

_____

_____

_____

Thoughts

_____

_____

_____

_____

Name & Relationship

_____

_____

_____

Wishes

_____

_____

_____

Thoughts

_____

_____

_____

_____

Guest

Name & Relationship

_____
_____
_____

Wishes

_____
_____
_____
_____

Thoughts

_____
_____
_____
_____

Guest

Name & Relationship

_____
_____
_____

Wishes

_____
_____
_____
_____

Thoughts

_____
_____
_____
_____

Guest

Name & Relationship

_____
_____
_____

Wishes

_____
_____
_____
_____

Thoughts

_____
_____
_____
_____

Name & Relationship

_____
_____
_____

Wishes

_____
_____
_____
_____

Thoughts

_____
_____
_____
_____

Guest

Name & Relationship

_____

_____

_____

Wishes

_____

_____

_____

_____

Thoughts

_____

_____

_____

_____

Guest

Name & Relationship

_____

_____

_____

Wishes

_____

_____

_____

Thoughts

_____

_____

_____

Name & Relationship

_____

_____

_____

Wishes

_____

_____

_____

_____

Thoughts

_____

_____

_____

_____

Guest

Name & Relationship

_____

_____

_____

Wishes

_____

_____

_____

Thoughts

_____

_____

_____

_____

Guest

Name & Relationship

_____

_____

_____

Wishes

_____

_____

_____

_____

Thoughts

_____

_____

_____

_____

Guest

Name & Relationship

_____
_____
_____

Wishes

_____
_____
_____

Thoughts

_____
_____
_____
_____

Guest

Name & Relationship

_____
_____
_____

Wishes

_____
_____
_____
_____

Thoughts

_____
_____
_____
_____

Name & Relationship

_____

_____

_____

Wishes

_____

_____

_____

Thoughts

_____

_____

_____

_____

Name & Relationship

_____

_____

_____

Wishes

_____

_____

_____

Thoughts

_____

_____

_____

Guest

Name & Relationship

_____

_____

_____

Wishes

_____

_____

_____

_____

Thoughts

_____

_____

_____

_____

Guest

Name & Relationship

_____

_____

_____

Wishes

_____

_____

_____

_____

Thoughts

_____

_____

_____

_____

Name & Relationship

_____

_____

_____

Wishes

_____

_____

_____

Thoughts

_____

_____

_____

_____

Guest

Name & Relationship

_____

_____

_____

Wishes

_____

_____

_____

_____

Thoughts

_____

_____

_____

_____

Guest

Name & Relationship

_____

_____

_____

Wishes

_____

_____

_____

_____

Thoughts

_____

_____

_____

_____

Guest

Name & Relationship

_____

_____

_____

Wishes

_____

_____

_____

_____

Thoughts

_____

_____

_____

_____

Guest

Name & Relationship

_____

_____

_____

Wishes

_____

_____

_____

Thoughts

_____

_____

_____

Guest

Name & Relationship

_____
_____
_____

Wishes

_____
_____
_____
_____

Thoughts

_____
_____
_____
_____

Guest

Name & Relationship

_____
_____
_____

Wishes

_____
_____
_____
_____

Thoughts

_____
_____
_____
_____

Guest

Name & Relationship

_____
_____
_____

Wishes

_____
_____
_____
_____

Thoughts

_____
_____
_____
_____

Name & Relationship

_____

_____

_____

Wishes

_____

_____

_____

_____

Thoughts

_____

_____

_____

_____

Guest

Name & Relationship

_____
_____
_____

Wishes

_____
_____
_____
_____

Thoughts

_____
_____
_____

Name & Relationship

_____

_____

_____

Wishes

_____

_____

_____

Thoughts

_____

_____

_____

Name & Relationship

_____
_____
_____

Wishes

_____
_____
_____

Thoughts

_____
_____
_____

Name & Relationship

_____

_____

_____

Wishes

_____

_____

_____

Thoughts

_____

_____

_____

_____

Gift Log Tracker

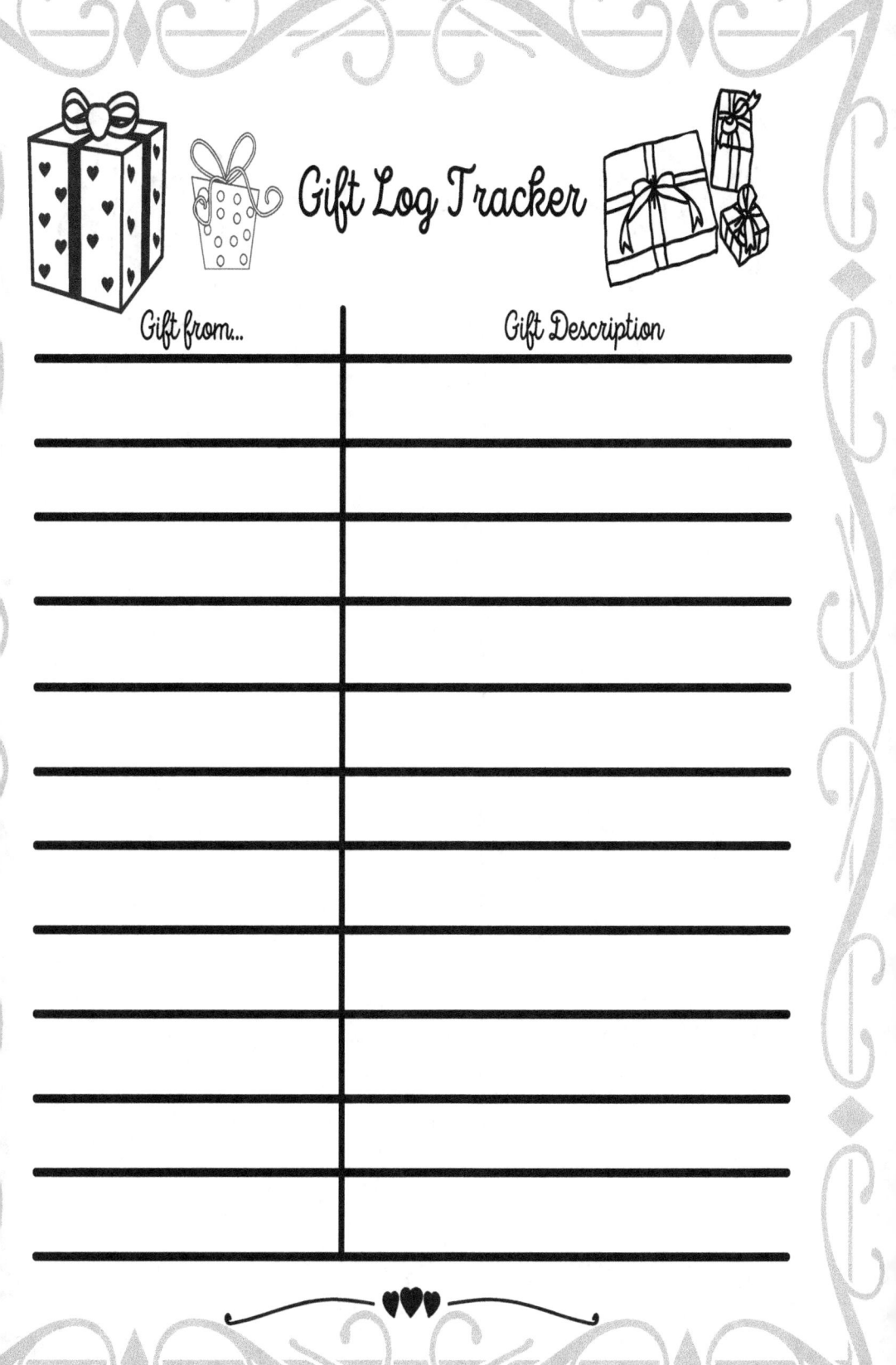

Gift from...	Gift Description

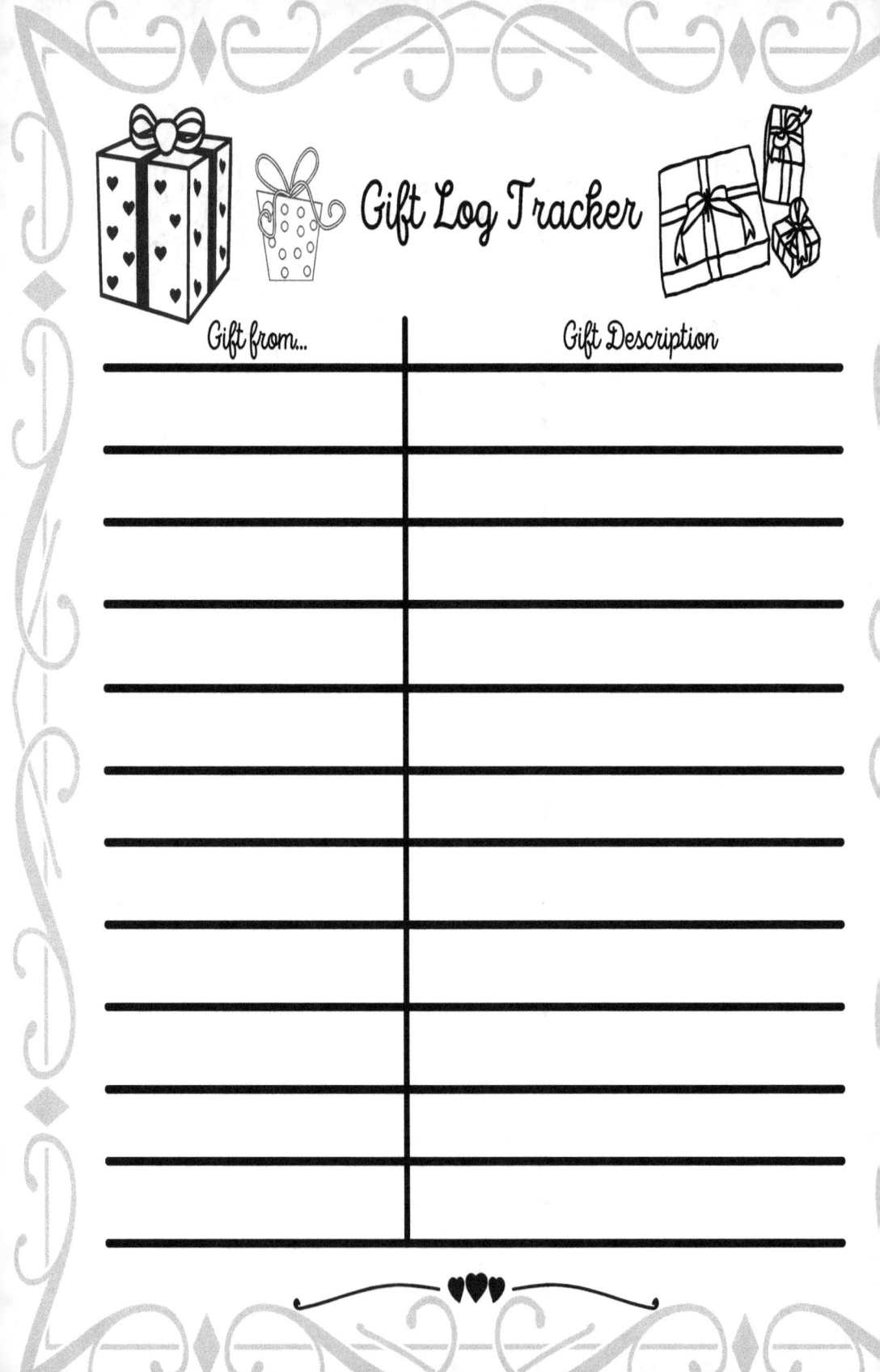

Gift Log Tracker

Gift from...	Gift Description

Gift Log Tracker

Gift from...	Gift Description

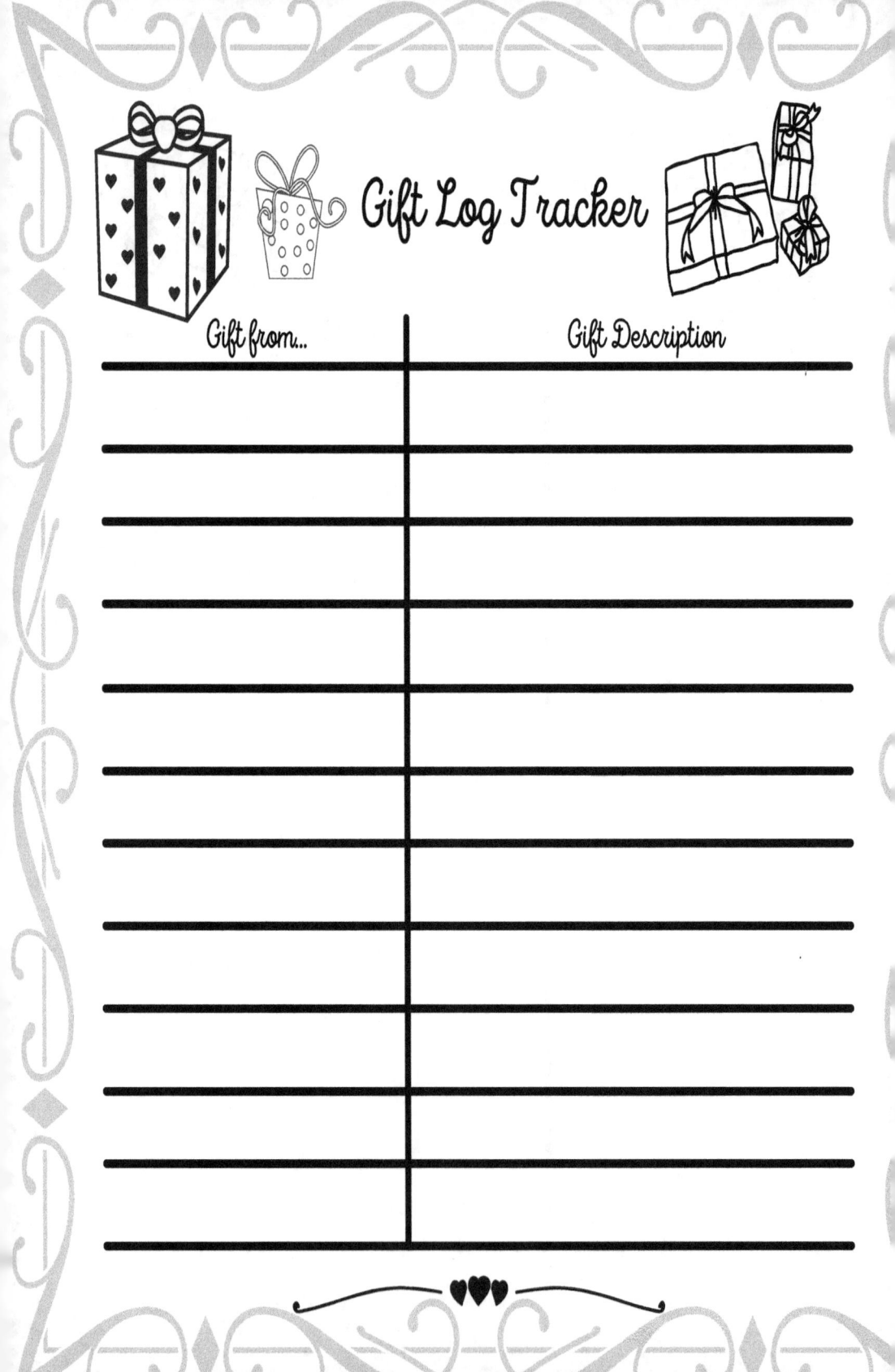

Gift Log Tracker

Gift from...	Gift Description

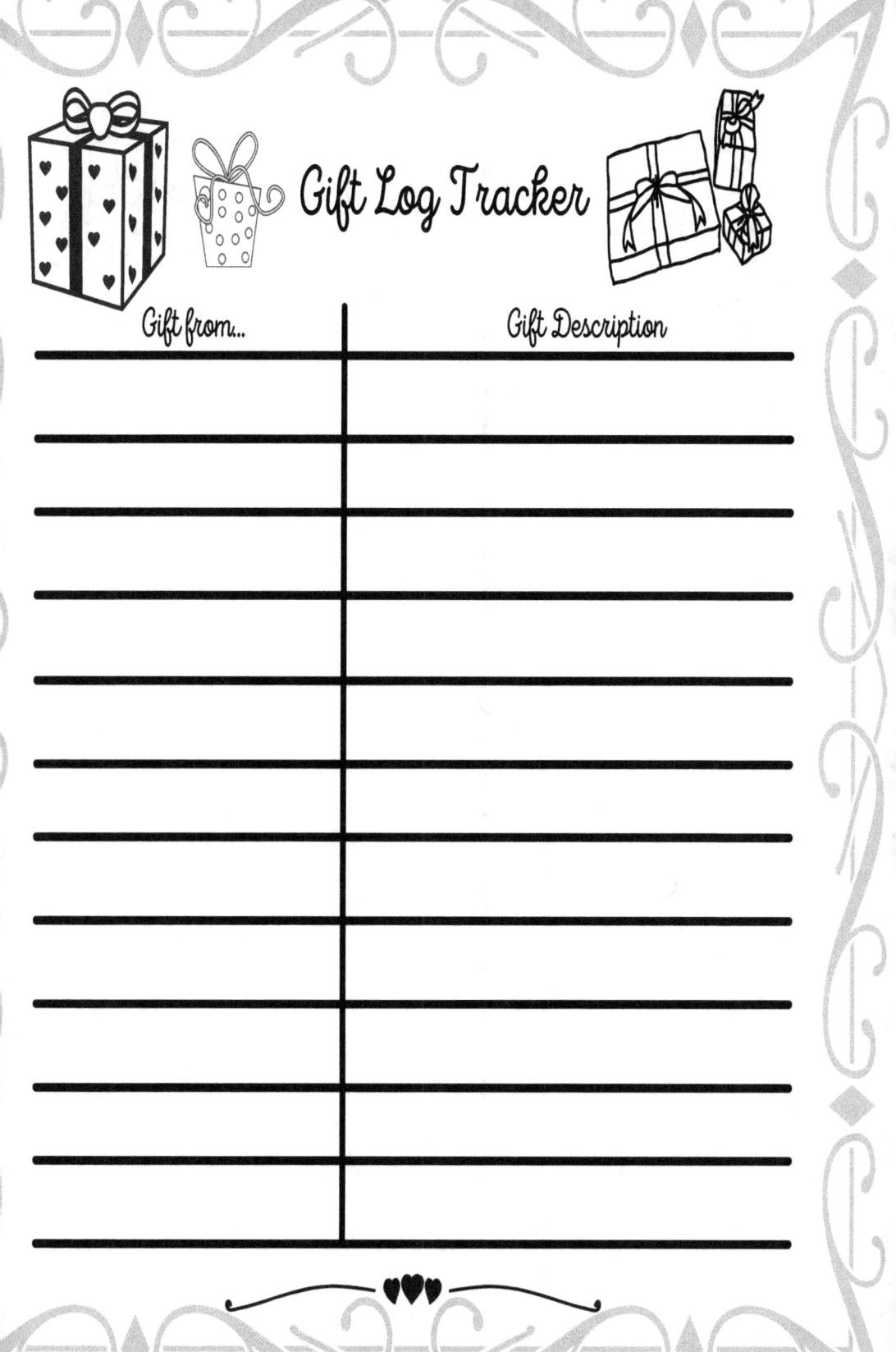

Gift Log Tracker

Gift from...	Gift Description

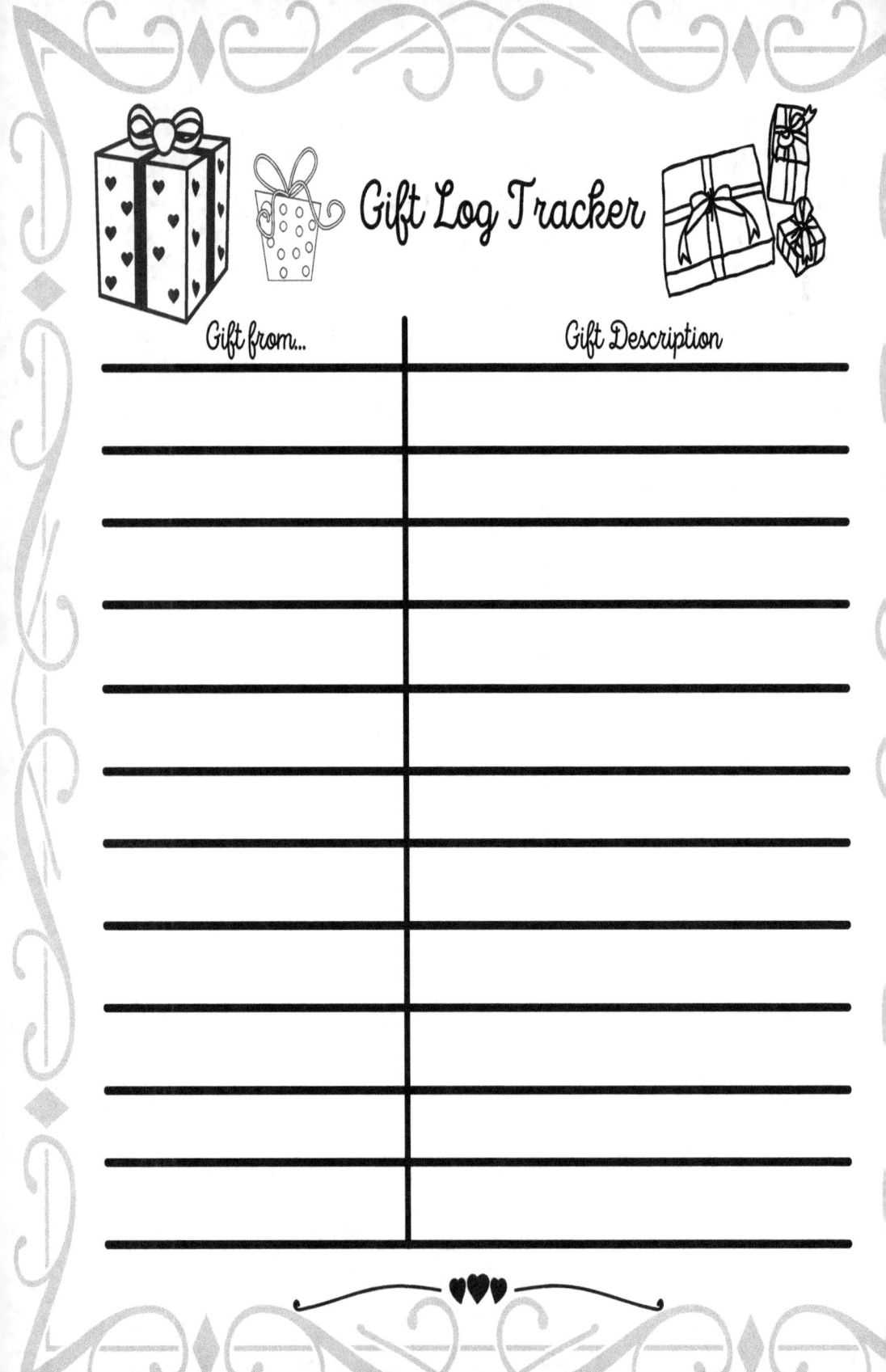

Gift Log Tracker

Gift from...	Gift Description

Gift Log Tracker

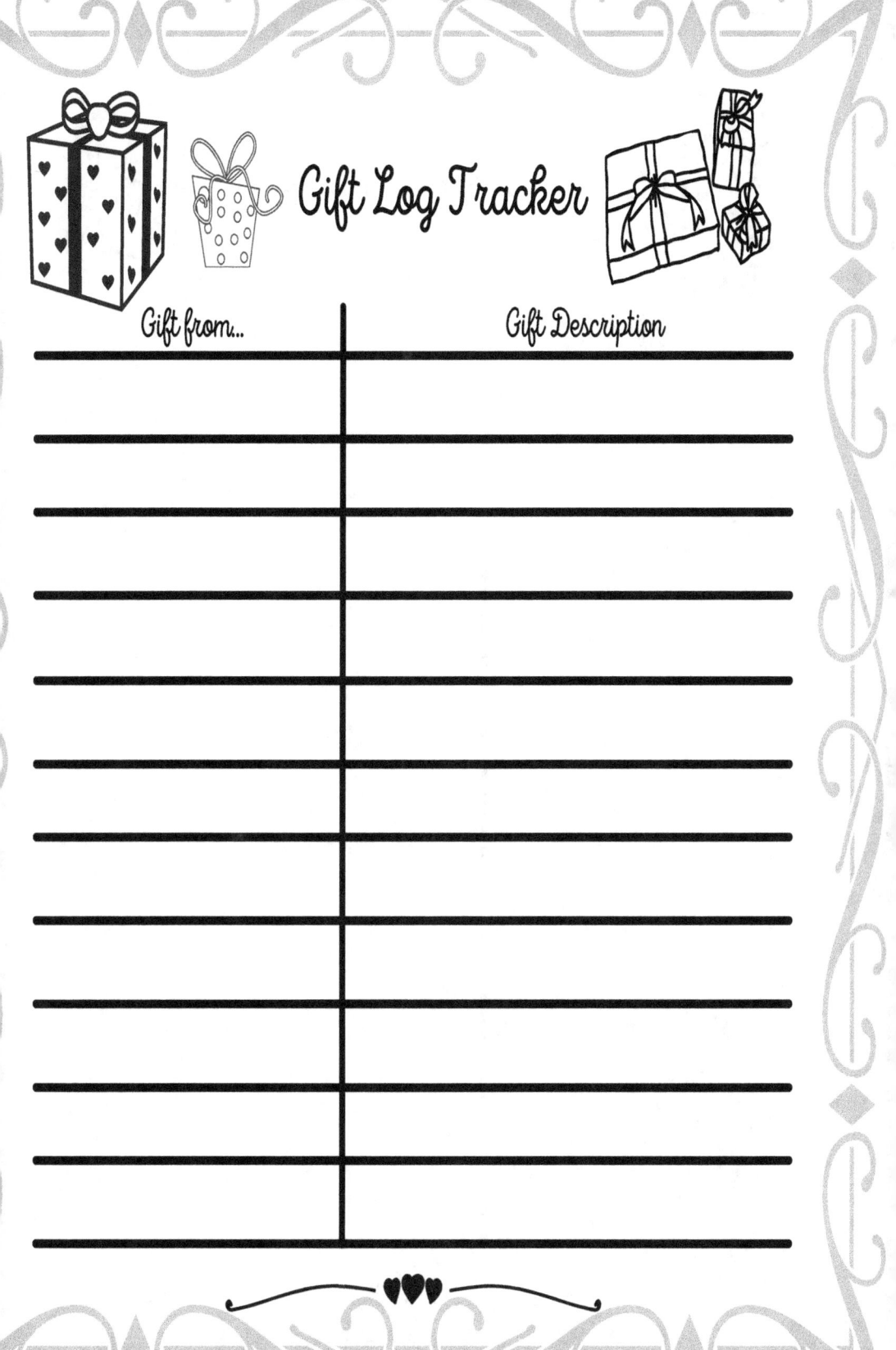

Gift from...	Gift Description

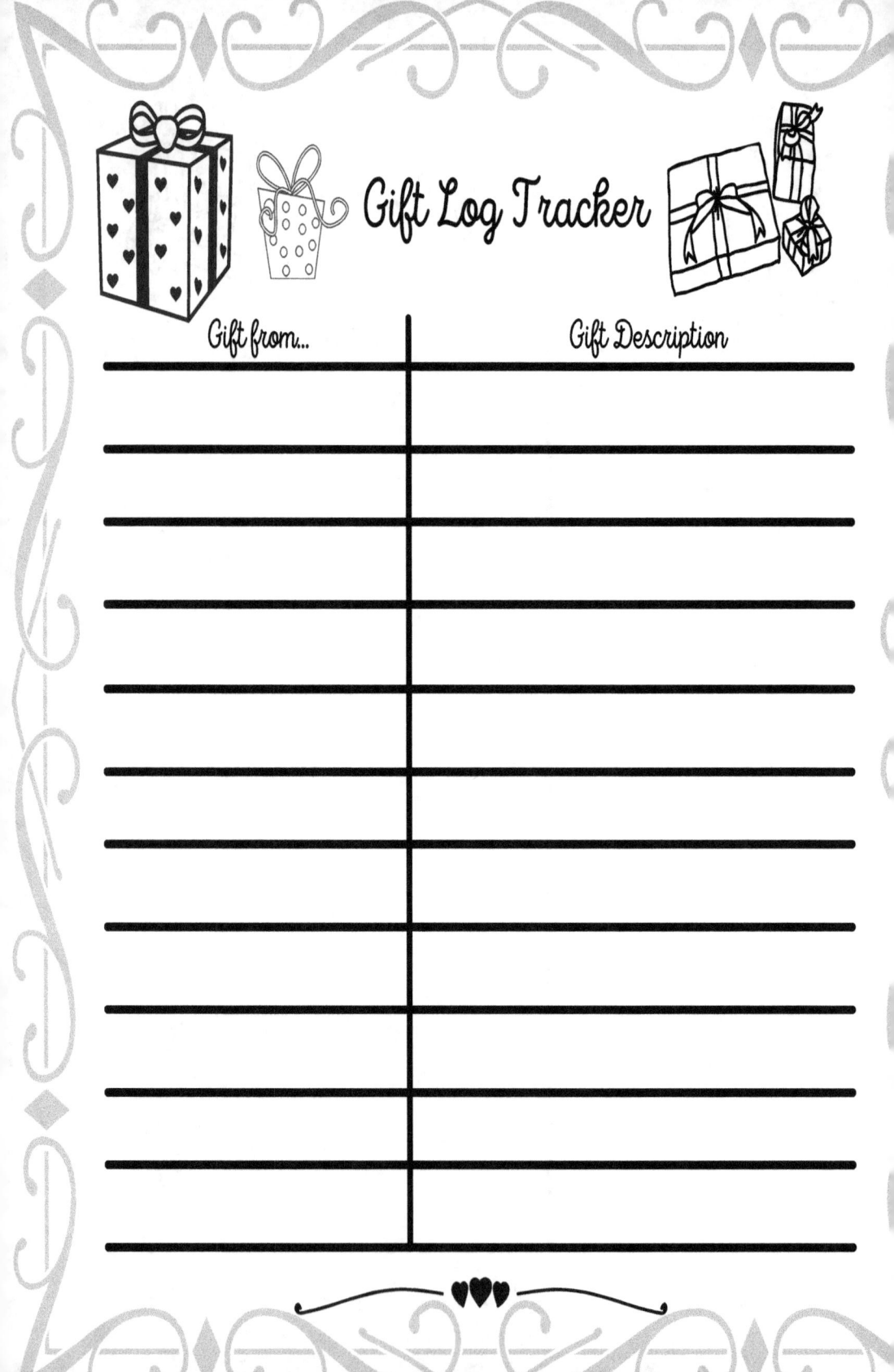

Gift Log Tracker

Gift from...	Gift Description

Thank You!

so much for trying our

Bridal shower Guest Book

We'd love to hear from you!

If you've found this to be a good book please
support us and leave a review.

If you have any suggestions or issues with this book, or if
you want to test some of our latest guest books
please email us.

Send email to:

pickme.readme@gmail.com

www.ingramcontent.com/pod-product-compliance
Lightning Source LLC
Chambersburg PA
CBHW071015120626
46546CB00003B/1095